IN PARLIAMENT 1939–50
The effect of the War on
the Palace of Westminster

A view of the Commons on 7 May 1940 during the debate which led to the resignation of the Prime Minister, Neville Chamberlain.
Mr. Chamberlain and Winston Churchill can be seen on the Government front bench and Lloyd George and Clement Attlee among the Opposition. This chamber, designed by Charles Barry, was first occupied in 1852. (From a painting by John Worsley—copyright *Life* Magazine)

HOUSE OF COMMONS
LIBRARY DOCUMENT No. 20

General Editor: Chris Pond

IN PARLIAMENT 1939–50
The effect of the War on the Palace of Westminster

Jennifer Tanfield

Assistant Librarian
House of Commons

LONDON: HMSO

HMSO publications are available from:

HMSO Publications Centre
(Mail and telephone orders only)
PO Box 276, London SW8 5DT
Telephone orders 071-873 9090
General enquiries 071-873 0011
(queuing system in operation for both numbers)

HMSO Bookshops
49 High Holborn, London, WC1V 6HB   071-873 0011 (Counter service only)
258 Broad Street, Birmingham, B1 2HE   021-643 3740
Southey House, 33 Wine Street, Bristol, BS1 2BQ   (0272) 264306
9–21 Princess Street, Manchester, M60 8AS   061-834 7201
80 Chichester Street, Belfast, BT1 4JY   (0232) 238451
71 Lothian Road, Edinburgh, EH3 9AZ   031-228 4181

HMSO's Accredited Agents
(see Yellow Pages)

and through good booksellers

Contents

Illustrations

Foreword
by Mr Speaker

IN THE DARK DAYS OF THE WAR, WHEN BRITAIN ALONE fought a continent overrun by the Axis powers, the building in which the House of Commons sat was destroyed by a chance visit from a German bomber.

A free Parliament is the proudest symbol of a democracy, and if anything, I think the pictures of the familiar Chamber a mass of rubble, twisted girders, and broken arches, made the British people even more aware than they were before of the mortal threat that Hitler posed to the tolerant and fair-minded way of life they enjoyed. And the picture of Churchill (on the front of this book) standing defiant among the ruins of the Chamber that even then he had debated in for more than 40 years, must have steeled our resolve to have away with the evils of Nazism once and for all.

You can destroy a man's house, but in doing so you may well preserve or strengthen his spirit. And so the House of Commons moved over the road, and on the next sitting day after the destruction of its Chamber turned, exactly as scheduled, to such matters as the Cannock Urban District Council Bill, pigswill collection, the Glen Affric dam and canteens at coal mines – the very stuff of democracy. The destruction of its meeting place interfered not one whit with the continuity of its routine business; nor with its much wider resolve to prosecute the War to a successful conclusion.

This book, written by Jennie Tanfield, herself not born when the destruction of the Chamber took place, is a fine appreciation of the wartime and austerity years here at Westminster. Its images evoke superbly those times of such great sadness and of such great spirit. I hope parliamentary colleagues of today and of the future will read it with great pride and great humility.

Bernard Weatherill
Speaker
March 1991

Introduction

THE REDISCOVERY IN THE HOUSE OF COMMONS
Library during 1990 of two albums of fine, officially commissioned,
photographs showing the effect of the wartime bombing on the
Palace of Westminster and the preparation of Church House to provide
debating chambers for both Houses of Parliament, led to the decision to make
the photographs available to a wider audience by means of an exhibition in the
Palace of Westminster and this accompanying document.

On the night of 10–11 May 1941 the House of Commons Chamber was
entirely destroyed by fire and the roof of Westminster Hall set alight. It was
therefore agreed that the exhibition 'In Parliament 1939–50' should be staged
close to the fiftieth anniversary of that bombing raid.

As work on preparing the exhibition began, it rapidly became clear that
there were numerous photographs and records in the offices of the
departments of the two Houses of Parliament, as well as relevant contempor-
ary accounts of life at Westminster during the war and its aftermath. The
principal problem, both in compiling the exhibits and writing this document,
has been to produce a small selection from all the fascinating items available.
In view of the wealth of material at Westminster it was decided to confine the
selection to that material, ignoring valuable pictures and records in other
archives such as the Imperial War Museum, the Public Record Office, and
Churchill College, Cambridge.

The author is grateful for the help she received from the staff of the
House of Lords Record Office, especially Lady Wedgwood, who first
suggested an exhibition and gave generously of her time and advice. Thanks
are also due to Hugh Farmer, formerly a senior member of the Clerk's
Department, who wrote with details of his role in planning the proposed
evacuation to Stratford-upon-Avon; to Baroness Elliot of Harwood who gave
tea and the benefit of her memories of 1941 and after; to Baroness Hylton-
Foster, whose father Col. Clifton Brown (later Viscount Ruffside) was
Speaker from 1943 to 1951, and who herself served as a Red Cross nurse in the
Palace; to Major Ron McDuell, son of Superintendent (later Commander)
McDuell, the fire officer in charge on 11–12 May 1941, who lent objects for the
Exhibition and copies of letters to his father; and to David ('Dusty') Millar,
Superintendent McDuell's driver, who was in the Palace on 10–11 May and
was probably the last person to stand in the old House of Commons Chamber.

Gratitude is also owed to Malcolm Hay, Curator of Works at the Palace;
Michael Cummins and Philip Wright, Serjeant at Arms Department; John
Arnold, House of Commons Postmaster; David Jones, House of Lords
Library; Adam Spencer, Records Officer London Fire and Civil Defence
Authority; Rosamund Coates of the Research Division of the House of
Commons Library. Chris Pond, also of the Commons Library, gave help and

encouragement and edited this volume. Fred Stubbs of HMSO Graphic Design has to be thanked for his work on the presentation of the document.

Thanks are due to Rt Hon Paul Channon MP, for permission to reproduce extracts from his father's diaries, to A P Watt Ltd, Crystal Hale, and Jocelyn Herbert, for permission to reproduce an extract from A P Herbert's *Independent Member*, and to various copyright holders for permission to reproduce photographs. These are acknowledged individually in photograph captions.

With the efflux of time, it has been impossible to contact every owner of copyright material republished here, although we made every effort to do so. For any unwitting infringement, we apologise.

Any errors or significant omissions are the sole responsibility of the author.

Chapter 1

How Parliament functioned

Locations

IN A MINUTE OF 22 OCTOBER 1940 TO SIR EDWARD BRIDGES (later Lord Bridges), Secretary to the Cabinet, the Prime Minister, Winston Churchill, wrote:

> 'I have already asked for alternative accommodation for Parliament, but no satisfactory plan has yet been made. The danger to both Houses during their Sessions is serious, but it is only a question of time before these buildings and chambers are struck. We must hope they will be struck when not occupied by their Members. The protection provided below the Houses of Parliament is totally inadequate against a direct hit. The Palace of Westminster and the Whitehall area is an obvious prime target of the enemy, and I daresay already more than fifty heavy bombs have fallen in the neighbourhood. The Cabinet has already favoured the idea of a trial trip being made by the House of Parliament in some alternative accommodation. I propose to ask for an Adjournment from Thursday next for a fortnight, by which time it is hoped some plan can be made in London for their meeting'[1]

The 'alternative accommodation' was Church House, Westminster. This was a modern building, with a stronger structure than the Palace of Westminster. It had been opened by King George VI on 10 June 1940. Although a bomb fell on Church House on 14 October 1940, destroying the assembly hall, this was taken as proof of the building's ability to withstand a direct hit. Sir Percy Harris (Liberal Chief Whip 1935 to 1945) says[2] that 'the Office of Works had converted in five days a large room to something like a replica of the old chamber in which the House of Commons met before it was burnt down in 1834'.

On 7 November 1940, both Houses met at Church House for the first time. The House of Commons Library has an album of photographs showing Church House being prepared for Parliament. It is assumed that these photographs date from the autumn of 1940. A selection from the album is reproduced on pages 3–4. The House of Lords sat in the Hall of Convocation and the Commons in the Hoare Memorial Hall, where a tablet commemorates their occupation. In the Commons Chamber the Hansard reporters sat on a low platform behind the Speaker, sharing the space with Ministers' officials and Parliamentary draftsmen.[3]

Church House was made an annexe to the Palace and the meeting places of the two Houses were therefore technically unchanged. The House of Commons Journals, which were not published until the end of the war (after the ban on disclosure of the place of sitting had been lifted), record that on particular days the House was sitting at 'the Annexe' and a note on the verso of the title page of the relevant volumes explains that the Annexe was Church House. Commons and Lords Hansard (the Official Report) and the House of

Lords Journals (which were published throughout the war) make no reference to the place of sitting.

Chips (Sir Henry) Channon, in his Diaries[4] describes the November 1940 meeting as follows:

> '7 November
> A dreadful day started with the House of Commons meeting for the first time in its new premises which Winston had dubbed 'The Annexe' – a large building astonishingly well arranged, many Members turned up early to watch the proceedings: it is the first time since the big fire of 1834 that the Commons have met anywhere except at Westminster ... The Speaker was enthroned under his usual canopy, the Serjeant-at-Arms on a camp chair at the Bar; Members found places as nearly as possible equivalent to where they usually sat at Westminster. The Hall was not too crowded, but the acoustics are indifferent and there was noise and muffled excitement, and ministers tumbling over one another. Winston watched the confusion with amusement. The atmosphere was gay, almost like the Dorchester. Outside in the cloisters, however, I ran into several clerics who seemed indignant that their building should have been taken for such lay purposes as law making. Proceedings followed their usual course with surprising ease. So strong is tradition among members of Parliament that all the usual forms and customs were observed.'

The moves to Church House were kept secret. Preparations for sittings were made overnight, and when the Members of the two Houses turned up for sittings in the Palace they were met by policemen at the gates and redirected to Church House.[5]

Both Houses sat in Church House again on 19 November 1940. On 20 November Parliament was prorogued in the Palace of Westminster, then on 21 November the King, accompanied by the Queen, opened the new Session in Church House. Guy Eden, a member of the Press Gallery, tells an amusing story of that State Opening:

> 'The building [Church House] was not designed as a Parliament House, and although those responsible made a wonderful job of the transformation, it had many inconveniences. Not the least of them was that war-damage had made it necessary to take somewhat circuitous routes from one part of the big building to another.
>
> When the King performed the only Royal Opening ceremony actually carried out in Church House, this led to an incident which, although it greatly amused those who knew about it at the time, has never hitherto been published.
>
> 'The House of Lords were sitting in a room about the size of a modest drawing-room – the doors were so narrow that the King and Queen, hand-in-hand as tradition dictates, were unable to enter side by side – and fewer than 100 people were present on this historic occasion. I was fortunate enough to be one of them.
>
> 'The House was far from the Commons' Chamber, and the way from one to the other was winding and puzzling.
>
> 'Black Rod, the Lords' official Messenger, was dispatched to "command" the Commons to attend on the King. Off he went, and, according to custom, everywhere he appeared the police cried: "Make way for Black Rod!" That official [...], new to the building, completely lost himself in the maze, and everytime he approached a policeman to ask the way, he was received with at stentorian shout of: "Make way for Black Rod!" which sent him, blushing and silent, on his way.

Hoare Memorial Hall, Church House, set up for meetings of the House of Commons

Hall of Convocation, Church House, set up for the meetings of the House of Lords

The Members' Smoking
Room and Lounge in
Church House

Vote Office and telephones
in Church House

'Eventually, he, by accident, found the Members' Lobby of the Commons, and, with a sigh of relief, stepped forward briskly to give the traditional three hearty raps on the door, to demand admittance.

'But a watchful door-keeper leaped forward just as the heavy Rod was about to descend, and arrested the arm of the bewildered emissary of their Lordships. The Commons' official silently raised a heavy curtain that covered the door – and there, right where the crashing blow would have landed, showed a pane of glass! Exactly what would have been the effect inside the silent Chamber, had Black Rod smashed the glass, can only be left to the imagination.'[6]

Anthony Eden (later Lord Avon) remembered, 'One thing about Church House which used to distress me very much. The Front Benches were very much too close to one another and the consequence was that we saw very too much of one another'[7].

The Houses continued to sit in Church House from time to time, e.g. in December 1940 and in April 1941 (for precise dates see Appendix I). B. H. Coode, Clerk of Public Bills, in an article published in 1945,[8] wrote: 'Although the building might be considered safer because of its closer and stouter construction, and although it was not easily identifiable, it never became popular with Members of Parliament; its topography was found to be inconvenient and difficult to master; there were no proper means of reference to books and papers. The result was a constant running to and fro between Church House and the Palace of Westminster, which made it often difficult to know where anybody was, Members or staff. Members themselves preferred the Palace of Westminster, and resorted to it for everything except the actual sitting of the House'.

Confirmation of the reaction of Members to Church House comes from A. P. Herbert, 'grateful though we were to our episcopal hosts, nobody was happy there. The buiding, we thought, was cold and uncomfortable. We missed our warm panelling and spacious lobbies, our library and smoking room. When we went back to our own place, all were agreed, I think, that the risk of bombs was better than the home of Bishops'.[8A]

In his article, Coode recorded that:

'Before war broke out in September, 1939, a plan had been evolved for the evacuation of Parliament from London to another place, which was kept secret. Billets for Members of both Houses were settled; transport, which involved in some cases railheads to which parties were to be conducted, were detailed; a certain amount of office baggage was kept packed in readiness for any emergency. The place selected – which is no longer a secret – was Stratford-on-Avon.'

It was planned that the House of Commons should sit in the theatre and the House of Lords in the Conference Hall. Hugh Farmer, a member of the Clerk's Department of the Commons, who retired as Clerk Administrator in 1972, wrote to the author with details of his duties concerning the evacuation – which was code-named 'HK'. Farmer, together with Captain Jagger, Head of the Admission Order Office, was sent to Stratford on two occasions lasting several days in September 1940 to arrange sleeping accommodation for Members and staff. In Farmer's words, 'We were given lists of houses in practically every road in Stratford and some better ones outside. We spent days trudging up and down inspecting every house. They were worthy two or three bedroom houses, perfectly clean and comfortable, but pretty small rooms. We quickly come to the decision that Members could be made to sleep in double rooms, but not in double beds!! Even so it was impossible to find beds for all, but we just hoped they would not all come. We lived with the nightmare possibility for over two years but by then the government had decided never to move'. Peers were to stay in the Falcon and Shakespeare Hotels.

A. P. Herbert remembered 'receiving a mysterious packet of secret instructions and labels. No destination was named, and I have no notion where we were to go'.[8A]

As recorded by Arthur Baker, chief of the parliamentary staff of *The Times* throughout the war, 'long and complicated instructions' were issued to all those due to be evacuated. 'The instructions envisaged two plans. "Black Plan A" was to be put into operation if Paddington Station was usable; "Black Plan B" if it was not. The hand-luggage and personal-baggage labels were most elaborate. Our code letters were HK and the collecting station for personal luggage was Reading. We were each issued with a travelling pass, franked by the stamp of the Serjeant at Arms'. (A travel warrant to HK is illustrated. Copies of the instructions issued are filed in the House of Lords Record Office.[9])

'As soon, however, as enemy bombing started in the summer of 1940 the whole scheme with regard to Stratford-on-Avon began to fade into oblivion. There were obvious reasons for this. For one thing a landing in England fortunately did not happen, owing largely to the heroism of the Royal Air Force; the bombing of such places as Coventry soon made it apparent that no one place was likely in any wa to be more immune from bombing than another; any locality selected – Stratford-on-Avon or any other town – would undoubtedly be discovered by the enemy and therefore become a special target for the enemy air force. But more important than any of these considerations to Members of Parliament was their determination to remain where they were with the people of London and face the attack there'.[10]

Speaking in 1952, when paying tribute to King George VI, Col. Walter Elliot MP said:

> 'I remember well the spontaneous revulsion of feeling in the House when it was suggested that it should quit London, and I believe the same feeling was shared by the late King. We saw it through together, and it made a bond of unity which I believe reinforced even the great bonds of unity between the King and his people which existed before.'[11]

In case both the Palace of Westminster and Church House were severely damaged, other possible locations in London were identified. These included Lambeth Bridge House and Gladstone School, Willesden Green, both for the House of Lords.[12]

Details of the arrangements made for the meeting of both Houses following the destruction of the Commons Chamber in May 1941 are given in Chapter 4.

Times of Sittings

From 18 September 1940, following a debate in secret session on 17 September (during which the Prime Minister proposed a ban on the publication of dates and hours of sitting and a reduction in the normal number of sittings) the Commons adopted special hours of sitting: from 11.00am to between 3.00 and 4.30pm. This arrangement continued until 9 March 1945, although Harold Nicolson records[13] that in May 1944 there was another secret session on the hours of sitting, when an earlier return to normal hours was proposed but defeated.

For a period, from mid-October 1939, the Commons sat only on Tuesday, Wednesday and Thursday, but in February 1940 a five day week was resumed. During the war years there were no long summer recesses; the Commons continued to meet intermittently in August and September. In 1940 the Commons sat for 10 days in August, for 4 days in August 1941 and for 3 days in August 1942, 1943 and 1944. Publication of the usual annual sittings return, recording days and hours of sitting, was suspended until July 1945 and from 1940 to 1944 the hours of sitting and timing of Members' speeches were omitted from the Official Report *(Hansard)*.

Secret Sessions and Censorship

In the words of Herbert Morrison (later Lord Morrison of Lambeth)

> 'The House [of Commons] met in secret session during the war for one reason – and one reason only – to keep from the enemy information which might help him in the prosecution of the war'.[14]

Secret sessions had been held between 1916 and 1918 during the first world war and were readopted from 1939. Motions were agreed for either House to go into secret session either to discuss a particular named subject or for the remainder of the sitting without any reason being specified. Frequently part of a sitting was held in secret and the public were then readmitted. Many of the secret sessions dealt with the days and hours of meeting of the House – 28 were concerned with sittings. There were 37 other secret sessions, (3 of which also dealt with sittings and are included in the 28): a total of 62.[15]

A complete list of the secret sessions of the House of Commons is given in Appendix II and of the House of Lords in Appendix III. When a secret session was moved (by a Member 'spying strangers') the Official Report *(Hansard)* records:

SECRET SESSION

Question agreed to.

Notice taken, that Strangers were present.

Strangers withdrew accordingly.

Whereupon Mr. SPEAKER, *pursuant to Standing Order No. 89, put the Question,* "That Strangers be ordered to withdraw."

[The remainder of the Sitting was in Secret Session.]

The only official records of what was said or discussed in secret session are the reports which Mr Speaker usually published after a full day's debate was in secret. These were often very short, for example, 'The adjournment of the House was moved, and a debate took place on Home Defence and other matters'. On 31 March 1943 it was desired to show how Members had voted on an amendment to proposed hours of sitting and Mr Speaker, in his published report indicated that a division had taken place, gave the text of the question put (but not the subject under discussion) and the names of the Members who took part in the Division. Mr Speaker issued a brief report on 5 May 1942[16] when a breach of privilege in a previous secret session was alleged. A Member had been accused of disclosing a portion of the proceedings of the 23 April secret session. The House of Commons Journal[17] (published after the war) includes a fuller report of the incident, in which Mr Granville was accused of making a statement including the information that:

> 'Winston told us in Secret Session – but I understand we are all friends here
> and that no one will let this go any further – our position in the
> Mediterranean is absolutely disastrous – we have not one capital ship left in
> this sea'.

The Committee of Privileges, to whom the complaint was referred, found that the charge against Mr Granville had not been proved. An addendum dated April 1946 was added to the Commons Journal that on 19 December 1945 the Report of the Privileges Committee 'without the Minutes of Evidence' was ordered to be reprinted.[18]

On 19 December 1945, the House of Commons resolved that no proceedings held in secret during the wartime Parliament should any longer be secret. Authors could therefore include recollection of what was said in their memoirs and other writings. Three of Churchill's speeches were subsequently published as press releases and Charles Eade reconstructed five more speeches from notes in *Secret Session Speeches*.[19] A rather frank passage about de Gaulle omitted from one of the speeches reconstructed by Eade is included by Martin Gilbert.[20]

In modern times proceedings in Parliament are published in the press as well as in the Official Report and the Commons Journal.

> 'Special arrangements were made to ensure that useful information was not
> released to the enemy through Parliamentary debates. The Clerks of both
> Houses received copies of the Defence Notices, as well as the running

instructions issued to censors themselves. This enabled them to keep a close watch on the text of questions handed in at the Table and to advise Members if the wording of the question itself, or the likely answer, might give valuable information to the enemy. The Clerks also advised the Speaker during the course of debates if any damaging information was unwittingly disclosed: in such an event, the item was deleted from the Official Report and newspaper editors were requested not to publish it.'
(Extract from a Censorship Study Group report).

The procedure for applying censorship in the Commons was made clear on an occasion when the Military Censorship ordered the Press Gallery on no account to report a certain question which had been put by an MP. Mr Speaker Fitzroy informed the censor that 'there was only the censor of the House of Commons, namely Mr Speaker'[21].

William Barkley of the *Daily Express* recorded that to his knowledge 'on only four occasions throughout the war were instructions received from Mr Speaker that certain public statements should not be reported. An example was when an MP thoughtlessly revealed the position of every barrage balloon in Glasgow'[22]. Arthur Baker, the *Times* correspondent, explains in more detail how the system of voluntary censorship worked, using the example of a speech made in the House by David Kirkwood in which he revealed details of the bombing of Glasgow and Greenock. Baker, the Chairman of the Parliamentary Press Gallery, telephoned Sir Ralph Verney, the Speaker's Secretary. The Speaker, when consulted, agreed that the passage should be omitted, and the Editor of *Hansard* agreed. Not a word appeared in *Hansard* or any of the papers the next day.[23]

Membership of the House of Commons
There was no general election between November 1935 and July 1945, 'the longest period in modern times without a general election'[24]. Electoral registration was suspended after the outbreak of war and from 1940 onwards a Prolongation of Parliament Act was passed each year to remove for one year at a time the requirement for an election at least once every five years.

From the formation of the Coalition government in May 1940, there was an electoral truce, under which none of the parties to the coalition (the Conservative, Labour and Liberal parties) contested by-elections. Instead the local constituency asssociation of the party which had won the seat in 1935 nominated a candidate. Despite this truce, between the outbreak of war and the 1945 Dissolution there were 75 contested by-elections (and 66 uncontested elections)[25] and 13 seats changed hands[26]. Many of the contested elections involved candidates from the Common Wealth party, which was founded in 1942 by Sir Richard Acland (Liberal MP for Barnstaple) to contest all by-elections where a 'reactionary' candidate was standing. The Common Wealth party won three seats between 1943 and the 1945 general election and one at the general election. The number of independent and minor party Members rose from 9 in 1935 to 33 before the Dissolution in 1945.

The rules governing the holding of 'offices of profit' by Members were removed by the House of Commons Disqualification (Temporary Provisions) Acts which were passed each year from 1941 to 1944 and by the House of Commons (Service in His Majesty's Forces) Act 1939. It is estimated that in February 1941 about 200 MPs (including Ministers) were involved in some form of government service and another 116 were in the armed forces[27]. Absentees from the House included Malcolm MacDonald, who became High Commissioner to Canada in 1941, Sir Samuel Hoare, who did not appear in the House from spring 1940, when he was appointed ambassador to Spain, to 1944; and Sir Louis Spears, who was First Minister in the Middle East. 22 Members of the House were killed on active service.

During the Coalition government the Conservative, Liberal and Labour Whips worked together in a joint Whips office. A group of senior Labour Members sat on the Opposition front bench. Their spokesman was H. B. Lees-Smith from 1940–41, then F. Pethick-Lawrence and finally Arthur Greenwood from 1942–44. For a time a salary was paid to the chief Opposition spokesman but this was later suspended. The major criticism of the government came from a group of independent-minded Members. Earl Winterton describes how he and Emmanuel Shinwell and Hore-Belisha agreed on a joint presentation of views on defence, foreign policy and supply.[28] The relationship between Winterton and Shinwell was dubbed 'Arsenic and Old Lace' by Kingsley Martin of the *New Statesman*.

There are differing views of the effectiveness of the wartime House of Commons. Albert Viton, writing in an American journal[29], refers to 'the lamentable paucity of talent in the House ... hence also the deeply conservative atmosphere of the House ... The pre-war mediocrities who were placed in Parliament by a Central Conservative Association retarded the transformation of parliamentary machinery, if only because too many were too ignorant, too stupid, and too lethargic to realise the need for adjustment'. Ronald Butt, on the other hand, is far more positive. In his view, 'during the war years, the House of Commons remained a living and an important institution and it kept alive a spontaneous critical "opposition" to the government ... This, indeed was a "golden age" of the independent Member in Parliament in this century'[30].

A. P. Herbert, one of the best known of independent Members, reflected on the wartime Parliament in the following passage,

'Every Member, I suppose, did something else as well during the war (we met, for the most part, only three days in the week). But I admired, though I did not envy, those who still made the House their main place of duty, and attended regularly. It was a grim, frustrating, difficult duty. You could seldom say all that you meant or knew, because of the "public interest". If you applauded you were probably a "yes-man", or "hero-worshipper": and if you criticized you might be labelled ignorant, indiscreet, unpatriotic, or merely a "nagger". If, in spite of all, you felt impelled by conscience to say this or ask that, there were always the demons "Security" and "National Interest" eager to stop your mouth. The Speaker, through the Clerks at the Table, might refuse to accept your question – or the Minister to answer it. I do not think I ever suffered in this way myself. I am trying to speak fairly of some whose activities I seldom applauded at the time. They thought it right to go on being Members of Parliament, war or no war: I always, at least, admired their industry and courage, and now and then they had "something to show" at the end. Even if they had not, our ancient democratic system had something to show. For, in spite of Security and National Interest, many hard things could be said, and were. Mr. Churchill himself, at the height of his power and popularity, had to stand up and answer them. Hitler did not have to do that. But Hitler did not win.

Without the freedom to nag ("Security" and "National Interest" always excepted) the true solidity of Parliament and people would not have been so unanimously displayed. The few could chide, and so the many had a chance to cheer. Mr. Churchill and the Government Whips were always delighted when the Independent Labour Party (three or four Members only) insisted on "forcing a division" after some big debate: and the Prime Minister would laughingly thank Mr. Maxton for is opposition afterwards. For "a majority of 497 to 4" will catch the eye of the world when "carried unanimously" does not. How foolish – but how human!

The war-Parliament – Lords and Commons – deserved all the sincere compliments that Mr. Churchill used to pay it. It never surrendered all its rights: but it was content, on the whole, to nudge rather than nag, and was more of a help than a hindrance. Coming and going between their constituencies, their regiments, their ships, their battlefields or offices, and Westminster, the Members carried to the heart of things the feelings of the people and the Forces: and when some strong tide of opinion flowed in the country it surged up those channels to the Whips and the War Cabinet. Mr. Churchill did not have to summon the Gauleiters or the Gestapo to find out what the people were thinking.'[31]

Commentators are agreed on the valuable work of the Select Committees on National Expenditure, set up (as in 1917–18) 'to examine the current expenditure defrayed out of moneys provided by Parliament for the Defence Services, for Civil Defence, and for other services directly connected with the war, and to report what, if any, economies consistent with the execution of the policy decided by the government, may be effected therein'. One of the wartime innovations, which has become a permanent feature of parliamentary procedure, was the setting up of a Select Committee on Statutory Instruments to scrutinise the very large amount of delegated legislation being introduced, particularly under the Emergency Powers (Defence) Acts.

Chapter 2

Wartime Activities in the House

The ARP

NATIONALLY, THE ARP (AIR RAID PRECAUTIONS, LATER officially called Civil Defence) dated back to a 1924 sub-committee of the Committee of Imperial Defence set up under the chairmanship of John Anderson (later Sir John and then Lord Waverley) to consider air raid precautions. In 1935 a circular was issued to local authorities urging them to prepare plans, and then in 1937 the Air Precautions Act was passed. Despite official action, amongst the general public and also in the Palace of Westminster, interest in, and recruitment to, the ARP was at a low level until after the invasion of Czechoslovakia in 1938.

After the Munich crisis, steps were taken to organise ARP in the Palace of Westminster, and in 1941 the Defence (Palace of Westminster Fire Prevention) Regulations were made. The regulations required that from 30 May 1941, all male British subjects employed at the Royal Palace of Westminster perform fire-prevention duties. Firewatching started on 17 March 1941 and continued until 11 January 1945. In total 1,168 persons took part in the internal defence of the Palace.[1]

AIR RAID WARNINGS

On receipt of an air raid warning Members are requested to make their way immediately to the *nearest* refuge, as indicated by direction arrows on the notices posted in the corridors. These refuges are in various parts of the building.

If the House is sitting when an air raid warning is received, the Speaker (or Chairman) will at once announce " Air raid warning—sitting suspended ".

Air raid warnings will be made known by Police and Custodians who, in addition to calling out " Air raid warning ", will blow sharp blasts on their whistles.

CHARLES HOWARD,
Serjeant at Arms.

Amongst the firewatchers was Earl Winterton, later (1945–1951) Father of the House of Commons. His description of the organisation underlines the camaraderie and departure from the usual parliamentary hierarchy:

'During most of the war I was a fire-watcher at the House of Commons on certain nights of the week. I rejoiced, by reason of my seniority and knowledge of the Palace of Westminster, in the imposing title of Assistant-Controller, which I shared with another senior member and one of the senior officials who were each on duty on certain nights of the week. Our designation was less impressive than it seemed, as the real work was done by the Controllers, who were all members of the custodians' service of the House. The custodians are uniformed officials who supplement the Metropolitan Police in looking after the comfort and security of both Houses of Parliament and members. They are mostly ex-Service men of high character and fine war records. In complete accord with democratic principles, I obeyed promptly and explicitly the orders of my chief – the custodian who was Controller on my night of duty – during the hours of "black-out" whilst he, during the day, when we met, saluted me, in accordance with custom, and called me "My Lord". The fire-watching organisation of the two Houses of Parliament included Peers, MPs and members of the staff of all grades of the Palace of Westminster. We were a happy, friendly body in which all social distinctions were ignored. We owed much to the tact, ability and good humour of Captain Victor Goodman, one of the Clerks of the Lords, who was Chief Air Raid Precaution and Security Officer of the Palace of Westminster. I still remember with pleasure an excellent Christmas dinner we had in our canteen on Christmas Day, 1941.'[2]

Harold Nicolson was another of the MP fire-watchers. He recorded one of his duty nights in his diary for 6 October 1942:

'I go down to the House for fire-watching. I go to the post and am given my steel helmet, lamp and whistle. I then go to the Lord Chancellor's corridor where the truckle beds are . . . I then (10.20 pm) go upstairs and lay me on my truckle bed. I have army blankets which are none too clean. I do not undress. There are three other people in the room with me. I have the remains of my cold, and cough badly. I do not sleep. I hear eleven strike, and then one, and then four, five, six, seven. I then get up, fold my blankets, deliver up my lamp and whistle, and walk out into a lovely sunrise.'[3]

Extract from the ARP diary The official ARP diary held in the House of Lords Record Office indicates that blankets were a regular source of concern and there are a number of references to missing blankets.[4] Arthur Baker, the *Times* correspondent, was also a fire-watcher. He recounts that his group of fire-watchers often went to the House of Commons Library to read both before and after their supper in the staff canteen.[5]

Badge worn by the Home Guard, Palace of Westminster

The Home Guard

On 14 May 1940 the Local Defence Volunteers, soon re-christened the Home Guard, were formed nationally as a supplement to the regular army for the defence of this country. A parliamentary Home Guard company ('C' Company 35th London (Civil Service) Battalion, Home Guard) was formed, and took part in the fire-watching duties as well as manning a gun at the exit from Westminster Underground Station and participating in Home Guard exercises. They also provided an armed guard of honour at wartime State Openings of Parliament. Queen Elizabeth (the present Queen Mother) reportedly commented on this departure from the normal parliamentary rules about arms.[6]

ABOVE LEFT
Lord Strabolgi, Sir G. Shakespeare (MP for Norwich) and Sir Gordon Touche (MP for Reigate)

ABOVE CENTRE
Lord Strabolgi parading his men

ABOVE RIGHT
Victor Goodman (later Sir Victor, Clerk of the Parliaments), Edward Fellowes (later Sir Edward, Clerk of the House of Commons), Guy Eden (lobby correspondent) and Glenvil Hall (MP for Colne Valley)

BELOW LEFT
The Prime Minister inspecting the Home Guard with Sir D. Gunston (MP for Thornbury) in dark glasses

BELOW RIGHT
The Parliamentary Home Guard Unit was responsible for putting anti-tank obstacles at the end of Westminster Bridge

Sergeant Pusey (Speaker's Trainbearer) instructing in the Northover Projector

ABOVE
M.P. Price (MP for Forest of Dean) and L. Boyce (MP for Gloucester, later Lord Mayor of London)

RIGHT
Harry Charleton (MP for South Leeds) with four women auxiliaries

Munitions Factory

On 1 June 1945, a BBC Forces News Programme broadcast a short report revealing for the first time that a Munitions Factory had been set up within the Palace of Westminster:

> 'During the years of War, a secret Munition Factory has been working at high pressure right underneath the British Houses of Parliament. In the vaults, men over 70 and young girls have worked side by side with high parliamentary officials, Cabinet Ministers' wives, policemen and civil servants.
>
> The factory never stopped work, even when the "Imminent Danger" warning was sounded during the Flying Bomb attack last year. This underground workshop produced over a million items for one Ministry of Supply factory alone and work still goes on.
>
> Government Departments quickly found they could rely on the Westminster Munitions Unit, as it is officially known, to produce highly essential munitions with the greatest speed . . . and they are doing so now, for the Japanese War.'

The relatively short news item makes no reference to the great efforts of Members of Parliament and (particularly) of parliamentary officials which preceded the setting up of the factory. Initially in 1942, Members and staff had volunteered to work in nearby factories, but, as this conflicted with duties such as Home Guard, fire-watching and parliamentary commitments, a Palace of Westminster Munitions Factory was proposed. An underground vault containing maintenance workshops, situated beneath the Central Hall (or Lobby) was chosen. The passages radiating from the actual vault were designated for stores, paintshop, inspection and assembly shops, First Aid and other subsidiary departments.

Permission for the Munitions Factory had to be obtained from the Lord Great Chamberlain, who at the time was Lord Ancaster (described by Barnett Cocks as a 'personage virtually unknown to those who worked in Parliament'[7]). He let it be known in December 1942 via his secretary, Lord Esmé Gordon Lennox, that he would 'under no circumstances . . . allow this scheme to be carried out.' Lord Ancaster refused again in January 1943 but the organisers in Westminster, led by Sir Geoffrey Mander MP, appealed to Oliver Lyttleton (later Lord Chandos), the Minister of Production. Lyttleton wrote a personal letter to the Lord Great Chamberlain who finally gave written approval to the scheme on 1 February 1943. (Speaking later in a debate in the Commons, Lord Willoughby de Eresby, son of Lord Ancaster, said that it was almost a general rule of the Lord Great Chamberlain's office that any request was always refused the first time it was made, 'When it is made the second time, and is a reasonable request, it is always agreed to.'[8])

The 'Munitions Workshop' was run under the direction of the Ministry of Supply by volunteers recruited from Members and staff of either House and their friends. American Lend Lease machinery was installed. The engineer in charge, Mr. C. Donaldson, started work on 12 April 1943 and the unit became fully operable in December 1943. At the peak point in May/June 1944, 1,800 man and woman hours were being worked. Special canteen facilities were provided, which served 150 meals each day. The work was carried out in three shifts.

'The main item produced was a torque amplifier which was part of a predictor unit for mobile and stationary anti-aircraft guns. The amplifier was completed in time to be used to destroy flying bombs.

THE SPEAKER GOES DOWN TO THE VAULTS . . .

. . . and makes a speech of thanks and farewell to the workers in the Palace of Westminster munitions unit which is now closing down. Among other achievements the unit produced 220 secret instruments for submarines. —

ABOVE
The Munitions Factory

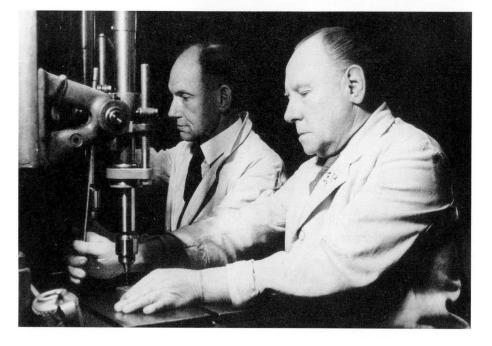

LEFT
Two munitions workers

A secondary item of production was the assembling (as distinct from manufacture) of detonator holders and priming fuses. This involved the inspection of all parts, their assembly and their despatch to the filling factories.'[9]

It is also recorded that over 2 million shell fuse parts were inspected for the Woolwich Arsenal Inspection Department and 95,000 special packing case fittings made as a sideline. Amongst those who volunteered for work in the unit were Mrs. D. Foot, Mrs. Sandys and Lady Nicholson.

As indicated in a parliamentary answer on 3 December 1945, the unit continued to operate until the end of 1945 to complete a contract for the Admiralty in connection with oxygen supply in submarines. 'The order was placed with the Palace of Westminster Munitions Unit because of the high technical standards they had attained on a previous Admiralty development contract.'[10] After closure, the tools were passed to Battersea Grammar School.

Chapter 3

Bomb Damage

THE HOUSES OF PARLIAMENT WERE DAMAGED BY AIR raids on fourteen different occasions, the most important being as follows:

On 12 September 1940 an oil bomb struck the West Front and started a fire, which was quickly put out.

On 26 September 1940 a high explosive bomb which fell into Old Palace Yard caused severe damage to the south wall of St. Stephen's Porch, the tracery of the great window in this wall, the War Memorial under the window, and the masonry of the West Front. The statue of Richard Coeur de Lion appears to have been lifted bodily from the pedestal but sustained only minor damage, the sword being bent.

On 8 December 1940 a high explosive bomb demolished the south and east sides of the Cloisters and did considerable damage to the other two sides.

The raid on 10 May 1941 was not a deliberate attack on the Houses of Parliament. At least twelve incidents are recorded on this night in various parts of the building, and three people were killed. The Commons Chamber was entirely destroyed by a fire which spread to the Members' Lobby and caused the ceiling to collapse. The roof of Westminster Hall was also set on fire. Part of the lantern and a considerable area of the roof boarding and rafters were destroyed, but the trusses do not appear to have suffered to any great extent. A small bomb or an anti-aircraft shell struck the Clock Tower at the eaves of the metal roof and destroyed some of the ornamental ironwork and damaged the stonework. All the glass in the south clock face was broken, but the clock and bells were undamaged and the chimes were broadcast as usual. The House of Lords was struck by a bomb which passed through the floor of the Chamber without exploding. The north side of Peers Court, the Government and Labour Whips' Offices, and a number of other rooms were destroyed.

On 22 January 1944, incendiary bombs set fire to the roofs of Westminster Hall and the Grand Committee Room without doing serious damage, and on 15 July 1944 a flying bomb which fell on St. Thomas's Hospital broke a large number of windows on the Terrace front.[1]

[Fell's *The Houses of Parliament: A Short Guide to the Palace of Westminster* 1950 Edition]

The two fine photographs at pages 23–24 show the effect of the September 1940 bomb which fell in Old Palace Yard. Firewatching staff stationed in Old Palace Yard were lucky to escape with their lives but some, including J.V. Kitto, the Librarian of the House of Commons, were injured.[2]

Damage caused by bomb on 26 September 1940

The 26 September 1940 bomb crater

The Commons Chamber after the 10–11 May 1941 bombing

RIGHT AND BELOW
**'The open air and a sort of
Tintern Abbey gaping
before me'**
(Harold Nicolson MP)

OPPOSITE
The 'Aye' division lobby

OPPOSITE ABOVE
Westminster Hall, although damaged, was saved

OPPOSITE BELOW
Star Court
None of the thirty firemen working here was seriously injured when the wall of the Chamber collapsed around them

The incendiary bombs which fell on the night of 10-11 May 1941 caused the greatest damage to the Palace. The summary which follows draws on a number of dramatic accounts of the events of that night and the role of Col. the Right Honourable Walter Elliot MP. Amongst these accounts are that in the official commemorative volume to mark the opening of the new chamber,[3] an article entitled, 'The night of May 10, 1941. From a Parliamentary Fire Watcher', published in a *Times* commemorative survey to mark the opening of the new chamber[4]; an account published in *London Calling*, the overseas journal of the BBC, by Robin Duff, a broadcaster attached to the London Fire Brigade and present in the Palace on 10 May[5] the prologue to the book *Westminster Hall* by Hilary St. George Saunders[6]; Librarian of the House of Commons from 1946 to 1950; William Sanson's *Westminster in War*[7] and a section in Christopher Jones's *The Great Palace*[8]. This last account quotes Col. Elliot's widow, Baroness Elliot, a member of the House of Lords.

The first bombs of the night fell at the Lords' end of the building, killing two auxiliary policemen stationed in a turret above the Queen's Gallery. A bomb then fell right through from a roof in the House of Lords to a basement kitchen, fatally injuring the resident superintendent. This bomb caused the ARP control room to be evacuated and put the lighting system out of action. It then became known that Westminster Hall was on fire, and later that the Chamber of the House of Commons was also alight. The London Fire Brigade had been summoned at 00.36 hours and Chief Superintendent McDuell, with thirty pumps and attendant firemen, was attempting to extinguish the Westminster Hall fires from the St. Stephen's end of the Hall. It was clear that it was going to be impossible to save both the Chamber and the Hall. Col. Elliot 'urged that every effort be made to save the Hall. It was, he said, of great antiquity and great historic interest. As a piece of architecture it was unique and worth any number of pseudo-gothic debating rooms not yet a hundred years old.'[9]

Col. Elliot then led the Fire Brigade, reinforced by firemen with a further sixty pumps initially summoned to deal with the Chamber fire, to the New Palace Yard end of Westminster Hall and, finding the doors of the Hall locked 'took a huge axe from a fire officer, and smashed the door open; pushed everybody through; rushed the water in and soaked the beams the whole way down, right down to the bottom. He told me that when he left Westminster Hall four or five hours later he was up to his knees in water.' (Lady Elliot's account as reported by Christopher Jones[10].) Talking to the author of this document in November 1990, Baroness Elliot suggested that it might be more accurate to say that her husband was 'almost' up to his knees in water. She emphasised that until Col. Elliot intervened the firemen had been at a loss as to what to do.

The official fire brigade report says '*Westminster Hall*. About 30-40 feet of roof damaged by fire. Empire Parliamentary Office (annexe) severely damaged by fire and most part of roof off, ceilings and contents under water'.[11]

Robin Duff records that some thirty firemen were fighting the fire in the House of Commons Chamber from Star Court when a delayed action bomb exploded inside the Chamber. The wall was hurtled into Star Court, which 'was filled with huge blocks of stone, and it looked as though there was not more than a square foot anywhere where a man could have lived. The only casualty among those thirty men was one badly sprained arm.'[12]

David Millar (known as Dusty) was Superintendent McDuell's driver and on 10 May had been given the job of searching the Palace (which he already knew) for pockets of fire. He was accompanied by Robin Duff and the Firemaster of Dunfermline. He told the author that after the first bomb hit the Chamber, he opened the door at the Speaker's chair end. Finding everything in order he shut the door and then 'wham' – the second bomb exploded. He believes he is the last person ever to stand in the Barry House of Commons Chamber.

Amongst the heroes of the night of 10–11 May was Police Sergeant Andrew Forbes. In 1936, as in 1990, the Victoria Tower had been scaffolded to allow work on the stonework to be carried out. Following the outbreak of war it was decided to leave this scaffolding in place. Having seen a fire bomb lodged at the top of the Victoria Tower and being unable to obtain the key giving access to the inside of the Tower, Sergeant Forbes, with a sand-bag over his shoulder, climbed up the scaffolding on the outside of the Tower 'to the 200 ft level where the planking was burning – a perfect target for the German bombers. He was just about to fling his puny sand-bag on to the flames when a jet of water played on them. Unbeknown to him, firemen had been going up *inside* the tower. Wearily he clambered down to street level. It took him 20 minutes each way.'[13]

A selection of the official photographs taken to record the damage to Westminster Hall and the Chamber of the Commons are included on pages 25–28. The scene shown by the photograph on p. 26 was memorably described by Harold Nicolson in the following passage:

> 'Diary 16th May, 1941
> I go to see the ruins of the old Chamber. It is impossible to get through the Members' Lobby which is a mass of twisted girders. So I went up by the staircase to the Ladies' Gallery and then suddenly, when I turned the corridor, there was the open air and a sort of Tintern Abbey gaping before me. The little Ministers' rooms to right and left of the Speaker's Lobby were still intact, but from there onwards there was absolutely nothing. No sign of anything but *murs calcinés* and twisted girders.'[14]

Rather quaintly, the official fire brigade report describes '*House of Commons*. A building of two floors about 100 × 60 feet (used as Assembly Hall and offices) and contents severely damaged by fire, most part of roof off.'[15]

Chapter 4

Arrangements after the May 1941 bombs

AS THE HOUSE OF COMMONS CHAMBER HAD BEEN totally destroyed, and the House of Lords Chamber damaged by the bomb which passed straight through it, both Houses moved to the Church House annexe and sat there from 13 May. However some weeks later the Prime Minister informed the House of Commons that, the House of Lords having placed their Chamber at the disposal of the Commons, his Majesty had directed that that Chamber should be made available for the Commons.

The House of Commons accordingly met in the House of Lords Chamber from late June 1941 until the new Chamber was opened in 1950, apart from a period during the 1944 flying bomb attacks when both Houses returned to Church House. The Lords met in the King's Robing Room, a fact which was kept secret between 1941 and 1944.

Photographs of the Lords chamber set up for the sittings of the House of Commons appear at p.32. To create a chamber as much like the destroyed Commons chamber as possible the Speaker's chair was placed at the north end of the room, the opposite end to the Throne and Woolsack. There was however no attempt to replace the red leather Lords benches with the usual Commons green benches, although microphones were installed to amplify the sound.[1] Drawings of Churchill speaking in a debate in the Lords Chamber and a wider view of a debate with Attlee at the dispatch box are shown at p.33. There is a film called *The Servant of the People* made in the late 1940s which shows a new MP, John Haire, the Member for Wycombe, in his first few days as a Member and which, (using actors to portray Members), features excerpts from Commons 'debates' in the Lords Chamber. To reach the temporary Commons Chamber the Speaker's procession had to pass through the Central Lobby. This proved such a popular feature that the practice was retained after the Commons moved back to its own new Chamber.

Earl Winterton, commenting on the Commons period in the Lords Chamber says, 'At first this vast gloomy building had a discouraging effect on many Members, to whom environment, when they are speaking, means everything: but, on the whole, the House adjusted itself very quickly to its new home as it had to its previous temporary home in Church House'[2].

Having donated their Chamber to the Commons, the Lords sat in the King's Robing Room. This room was much smaller than the Lords Chamber and had no gallery and no obvious place for Division Lobbies. Arthur Baker, the *Times* correspondent, describes the erection of an improvised gallery at one end, facing the Lord Chancellor on the Woolsack[3]. Wooden screens behind

The House of Lords Chamber arranged for sittings of the House of Commons

The Speaker's Chair at the north end of the Lords Chamber

Clement Attlee speaking in the Lords Chamber
(From an impression by Steven Spurrier)

Winston Churchill 'Spying Strangers' in the Lords Chamber
(From a drawing by Bryan de Grineau for *Illustrated London News*) (Illustrated London News Picture Library, *by permission*)

**A Lords debate in the
Robing Room**
(From a drawing by Bryan de
Grineau)

OPPOSITE ABOVE
**The Robing Room
arranged for sittings of the
House of Lords.**
The division lobbies were
behind the wooden screens

OPPOSITE BELOW
**The Robing Room
showing the gallery erected
at the west end**

the benches provided temporary Division Lobbies[4]. Alfred Bossom MP (later
Lord Bossom) commented that:

> 'On the whole, this temporary Chamber is simple and unpretentious, devoid
> of the grandiose carving and gilding of the Lords' own Chamber, yet it
> impresses the visitor as a typically British setting for the Lords' debates.'[5]

Photographs of the Robing Room set up for a sitting of the House of Lords
are shown at p.34 with, above, a drawing of the Lords in session. Speaking
during the debate in 1950 when the Commons paid tribute to the generosity
of the Lords in vacating their chamber, Clement Davies, Leader of the Liberal
Party, said 'I think the quality of their Lordships' Debates and of their
deliberations has been enhanced by the greater intimacy of the small
Chamber'[6]. Amongst the events that took place in the Robing Room was the
presentation to the King in March 1943 of the new Speaker, Colonel Clifton
Brown. Chips Channon records that this 'quaint, rather Alice-in-Wonderland
ceremony went on whilst a severe air-raid was in progress'[7].

The state openings of new sessions took place in the Robing Room from
1941 to 1944. As recorded above, the 1940 State Opening took place in Church
House, but following a request made by the King in 1944,[8] from 1945 to 1950
the Commons moved from the Lords Chamber to St Stephen's Hall for their
meeting before being summoned by Black Rod, and the King read his speech
in the House of Lords Chamber. A photograph of St Stephen's Hall arranged
for one of these occasions appears at p.37. The 1945 State Opening with the
Commons meeting in St Stephen's Hall took place on 15 August, 111 years
exactly from the Commons' previous meeting in St Stephen's.[9] For the State
Openings of the 1940s only officials and bishops attended wearing their usual

ceremonial garb; the King wore naval uniform and the Queen a day dress and hat. The peeresses also wore dresses and hats and the crown and other royal paraphernalia were brought in on cushions[10]. The *Illustrated London News* carried a picture and plan in its issue of 4 March 1950 showing the Lords Chamber set up for the Commons but modified to cope with the State Opening of that year. This 1950 State Opening was the first to return to full ceremonial with peers in scarlet robes again and the King robed and wearing the Crown.

Apart from making arrangements for the sittings of the two Houses, the authorities had to find temporary locations for other services which had been made homeless by the various bombs. The Members' cloakroom, which had been put out of action by the damage in December 1940 to the Cloisters, was transferred to temporary buildings in Westminster Hall. 'They were set up along its sides where for centuries the booksellers and seamstresses had plied their trades and gossiped with Pepys and Defoe, with Addison and Goldsmith and the *literati* of two centuries. The armoury of the Home Guard was also set here. These booths remained until 1950 when they were taken down in preparation for the ceremonies held to inaugurate the new Chamber of the House of Commons'[11].

The Central Lobby
'Beyond the hall lay a circular chamber with passages leading out of it in various directions, rows of telephone boxes on one side and a polished counter on the other. It struck me as being incredibly like the entrance hall of a second-rate hotel' (from *English Enigma* by Dorothy Jane Ward, an American visitor to the Palace)

St Stephen's Hall set up for Commons' meetings prior to State Openings

The Members' Post Office was affected by damage in the Commons Lobby, first from the December 1940 bomb in the Cloisters and then by the May 1941 bomb: it moved to the corridor between the Central Lobby and the Commons Lobby. A photograph of this temporary post office is shown on p.59. A line of Members' Telephones was provided in the Central Lobby.

The much loved 'Annie's' bar off the Members' Lobby, frequented by Members and the Press, was destroyed. For a time the Members' chess room was made into a bar open to MPs and members of the Press[12], but it was not until 1968 that a permanent replacement for the lost bar was provided in two rooms beneath the Members' Tea Room, the old site in the Lobby having become Opposition Whips' offices.

A. P. Herbert's impression of the Palace during the war was,

'It was a pretty grim place to work in, too . . . The "black-out", in such a building, was an almost impossible problem. A few hurricane-lamps on the floor were the only lighting of the great Central Hall, and they made it a lofty tomb of gloom. All the windows went in the early blitzes: the east side was all cardboard and sandbags, and you could not see the river from the Smoking Room. On the terrace was a Guards machine-gun post (of which I went in fear many nights on patrol, in the early days, when E-boats were expected in the Strand). Our favourite pictures and tapestries were taken away, and left depressing gaps. The Harcourt Room was full of beds for the A.R.P.: the lower corridors were anti-gas refuges. The Smoking Room closed earlier – very rightly – to let the staff get home before the blitz. And all the time there was the feeling that the things that mattered were happening elsewhere – a strange sad feeling for the proud M.P. and law-giver.'[13]

Chapter 5

Victory

ON 7 MAY 1945 THE ACT OF UNCONDITIONAL SURRENDER was signed by the Germans General Jodl and Grand Admiral Doenitz. The agreement was ratified on 8 May and hostilities in Europe came to an end at one minute past the midnight of 8 May. Prime Minister Churchill broadcast to the nation at 3.00 pm on 8 May and then made a statement to the House of Commons, after which the House proceeded to a service of thanksgiving in St. Margaret's Church, Westminster.

Chips Channon's vivid description of the occasion reads,

> '8 May   VE Day, at last
>
> At the House, Questions lasted interminably, and there was an atmosphere of expectancy in the crowded Chamber. Every seat was occupied; the Ambassadors were all present, peers queued up. At three o'clock, in the Whips' Room, I heard the PM make the official announcement over the wireless that the war in Europe was at an end. I then returned to the Chamber, but owing to the ovation Winston was having in the streets, he was delayed, and for a few embarrassed minutes we had nothing to do. Members, amused, asked desultory questions, keeping their eyes on the door behind the Speaker's chair. The Serjeant-at-Arms was in Court Dress, the Speaker wore his robes with gold braid, etc. (I have never seen this done before – although I suppose it was done at the Coronation.) At last Winston, smiling and bent, appeared, and had a tremendous reception. Everyone (except the recently elected cad for Chelmsford [ie E. R. Millington, the Common Wealth Member]) rose and cheered and waved handkerchiefs and Order Papers . . . . Winston smiled and half bowed – as he often does, and turning towards the Speaker, read out the same short announcement of the surrender of Germany which he had already given over the wireless. The House was profoundly moved, and gave him another great cheer; but his reception, even at a supreme moment like today, did not equal Mr Chamberlain's great ovation after Munich. Then Winston, in a lower voice, added his personal thanks and praise for the House of Commons and the Democratic System: some Members wept, and the PM moved that we repair to St Margaret's to offer thanks to Almighty God using the identical phraseology employed by Lloyd George in 1918. The Speaker headed the procession, followed by Winston, who walked with Arthur Greenwood. We walked through St Stephen's Hall and outside, where there was a terrific crowd, the sun was shining. There were bells, police carved a way for us, and we must have looked like a picture by Giovanni Bellini as we filed, 500 strong, into St Margaret's for a short and impressive service.'[1]

In a letter to his wife, Harold Nicolson set down his impression of the day.[2] He listened to Churchill's broadcast in New Palace Yard, where it was relayed through loudspeakers. Nicolson told his wife that tears came as the names of the Members who had laid down their lives were read out in the service of thanksgiving.

At midnight on 14 August 1945 the terms of the Japanese surrender were announced and Attlee, as Prime Minister, made a statement in the House on 15 August. Earlier in the day, the King had opened the first session of the new Parliament. As no definite news of the Japanese acceptance of the Allies' terms of surrender had been received by the afternoon of 14 August, two different versions of the King's Speech were prepared and signed by the King, an event without precedent.[3]

After the Prime Minister's statement the House proceeded to St Margaret's for another service of thanksgiving. At 11.00 am on 21 August 1945, at the suggestion of the King[4], based on the arrangements in 1918, both Houses assembled in the Royal Gallery to present Addresses of Congratulation on 'the victorious conclusion of the war'. In his reply, the King paid tribute to the armed forces, to those who gave their lives, to the people at home, to the women of Britain, to the support given by all parts of the Commonwealth and Empire and to the great and gallant Allies.[5]

The Speaker's Procession on VE Day

Chapter 6

The Rebuilding

IN OCTOBER 1943, THE COMMONS DEBATED THE QUESTION of rebuilding the Chamber. Churchill urged them to provide a small chamber, oblong not semi-circular, a House rebuilt on its old foundations, using as far as possible its shattered walls. Despite John Maxton's suggestion of a new parliamentary site some twenty miles from London, the House agreed to Churchill's proposals, and in December a Select Committee 'to consider and report upon plans for the rebuilding of the House of Commons and upon such alterations as may be considered desirable while preserving all essential features' was set up. Earl Winterton was the Chairman of the Committee and its clerk was Strathearn Gordon, later Librarian of the House of Commons. The Committee reported in October 1944: Harold Nicolson, in an essay in the *Spectator* in November 1944, noted that it would be beside the point to criticise the Committee for having recommended 'a 1944 imitation of an 1836 intimation of an assumed Gothic prototype', because the Committee's terms of reference had stipulated repetition of all essential features of the old Chamber.[1]

Sir Giles Gilbert Scott was recommended by the Committee as the architect of the new House and Dr Oscar Faber as the engineer. The House accepted the Committee's report after a lively debate, but without a division, on 25 January 1945. In this debate Churchill made a plea for the retention of the damaged archway into the Chamber from the Lobby 'as a monument to the ordeal which Westminster has passed through in the Great War, and as a reminder to those who will come centuries after us that they may look back from time to time upon their forbears who

> "—— kept the bridge
> In the brave days of old."[2]

To those in Westminster in the 1940s it seemed a long time before the new Chamber was under way. Arthur Baker recalled the deserted and desolate rectangle on which the Chamber had stood. 'The twisted girders, the charred and burnt-out woodwork, and the messes of brick and rubble had been cleared away. Weeds had begun to grow where formerly dark green leather seats had stood, and as I looked on this, day after day, I began to wonder if the new Chamber would ever be built.'[3]

Clearance of the Chamber site began in June 1945 and took approximately six months. An article describing the demolition problems and the careful preservation of the Churchill Arch and the Members' Corridor and Staircase appears in one of the commercially produced volumes to commemorate the new building.[4] The main contract was let by the Ministry of Works to John Mowlem & Co. The total cost of the new building was estimated to be £1,799,000 excluding £50,000 for furniture.[5] The outturn cost was £2,000,000 and £66,450 for furniture.[6]

OPPOSITE ABOVE
The laying of the Foundation Stone on 26 May 1948

OPPOSITE BELOW
Facing the Camera – Winston Churchill MP, the Lord Great Chamberlain (the Earl of Ancaster), Clement Attlee MP, the Dean of Westminster, Sir Giles Gilbert Scott (the architect), Charles Key MP, Earl Winterton MP, Herbert Morrison MP and Mr Speaker

RIGHT
Demolition

BELOW
Rebuilding
Work in progress on the new Chamber, 10 August 1948

The Foundation Stone, which can be seen today on the Chamber side of Star Court, was laid by Speaker Clifton Brown on 26 May 1948. A commemorative volume was produced[7] and a recording was made of the speeches by Attlee, Churchill, Winterton, the Speaker, and the Dean of Westminster. A copy of the recording still exists in mint condition in the House of Commons Library.

Although the House of Commons Chamber was so severely damaged, a certain amount of stone and timber was recovered. From this timber was made the present House of Commons snuff box (its predecessor having been destroyed in the post bomb fire), the handle of the trowel with which the Speaker laid the Foundation Stone and official souvenirs such as the gavel presented to the American House of Representatives. Numerous unofficial souvenirs were also made and sold to members of the public for the benefit of charities. A large quantity of pre-war stained glass also left the Palace and the present whereabouts of most of this glass is unknown. A charred Testament, recovered from the Despatch Boxes, was re-presented to the House in March 1991.

This gavel, made of timber from the bombed House of Commons, was presented by the Speaker of the House of Commons to the Speaker of the House of Representatives as a symbol of Anglo–American friendship on 17 February 1953

Chapter 7

Opening of the New Commons Chamber

THE NEW CHAMBER WAS OPENED ON 26 OCTOBER 1950. This was preceded by a message from the King delivered on 24 October inviting the Commons to occupy their new Chamber. The King's message was followed by a debate in which the Commons' address in reply to the King was agreed and then the House agreed on a message to the House of Peers thanking them for having placed their Chamber 'at the disposal of His Majesty for the occupation of the House of Commons'. In the course of his speech proposing the message to the Lords, Herbert Morrison (Leader of the House and Lord President of the Council) noted that many of the then members of the Commons would not have sat in any Chamber but the Lords Chamber.

BELOW
Inside the new Chamber

OVERLEAF
Prayers with Strangers present
26 October 1950, the opening of the new Chamber

Bryan de Grineau
New House of Commons 1950

On Thursday 26 October the Speaker took the chair at 10.15 am. At the wish of Speaker Clifton Brown, the traditional prayers, with which as usual the House began its proceedings, were said in the presence not only of Members but also, and contrary to the practice of the House, of strangers. The drawing on pp.46–47, taken from the *Illustrated London News* of 4 November 1950, shows this historic occasion. The Speaker welcomed the Speakers, Presiding Officers and other representatives of the Commonwealth and Empire who had come to join in the ceremonies. The Prime Minister, Clement Attlee, then made the first speech in the new Chamber, followed by the Leader of the Opposition, Winston Churchill. After speeches by the Leader of the Liberal Party (Clement Davies) and Earl Winterton, the Father of the House, the sitting was suspended just before 11.00 am.

The Members of both Houses and the overseas representatives then reassembled in Westminster Hall which had been cleared of scaffolding and temporary rooms and embellished with blue, red and gold furnishings to welcome the King and Queen. Loyal addresses from both Houses were read and the King 'graciously' replied. As the opening of the new Chamber was shortly before the opening of the new session (on 31 October), the King decided to drive to the Commons in a motor car and to wear morning dress. The Minister of Works, Richard Stokes, wrote to Sir Alan Lascelles (Private Secretary to the King) expressing his disappointment that the King had decided to come 'in a plain van'.[1]

Members entering the new Chamber on 26 October 1950

OPPOSITE
Presentation of addresses to King George VI on the opening of the new Chamber
(Illustrated London News Picture Library, *by permission*)

Opening of the New Commons

The text of the 24 October and 26 October speeches with detailed description of the destruction of the Chamber, the October 1950 ceremonies, a list of all the overseas gifts to the new Chamber, plus photographs of the ceremonies and the Commonwealth gifts are all included in the commemorative volume, *The New Chamber of the House of Commons in the Palace of Westminster. An Account of the Opening Ceremony 26 October 1950.*

Other volumes of commemoration were published, amongst them *The Times Survey of the House of Commons* which included a history of the building, accounts of the night of 10–11 May 1941 and details of the building and fitting out of the new Chamber. Another volume gives details of the companies and workmen who built and equipped the new House as well as detailed pictures ranging from heating and ventilation equipment to door handles.[2]

The Churchill Arch
'A monument to the ordeal which Westminster has passed through in the Great War'

Appendix I

Meetings at Church House

1940
7 November (Thursday)
19 November
(Parliament prorogued in the Palace of Westminster 20 November 1940)
21 November (HM The King opened the New Session)
10 December to 12 December
17 December to 19 December

1941
22 April to 24 April
29 April to 1 May
13 May to 15 May
20 May to 22 May
27 May to 29 May
10 June to 12 June
17 June to 19 June

1944
20 June to 23 June
27 June to 30 June
4 July to 7 July
11 July to 14 July
18 July to 21 July
25 July to 28 July
1 August to 3 August

Appendix II

Secret Sessions of the House of Commons 1940–1944

Session 1939–40
1939:   13 December
1940:   20, 27 June; 4, 9, 30 July; 17, 18, 19 September; 19, 24 October;
        6, 12, 13 November

Session 1940–41
1940:   21, 28 November; 12 December
1941:   4 February; 13, 26 March; 2 April; 14, 21 May; 11, 19, 25 June; 17, 23 July;
        6 August; 10 September; 9, 16, 23 October

Session 1941–42
1941:   12 November; 19 December
1942:   8 January; 11 February; 23 April; 5, 6 May; 25 June; 16 July; 4 August;
        15, 22 October

Session 1942–43
1942:   11, 24 November; 10 December
1943:   19, 21, 26 January; 31 March; 11 May; 4, 10, 23 November

Session 1943–44
1943:   24 November
1944:   24 February; 24, 31 March; 4, 18 May

Appendix III

Secret Sessions of the House of Lords 1940–1944

PROCEEDINGS IN SECRET SESSIONS OF THE HOUSE OF LORDS, 1940-1944.

Resolution.

Die Veneris, 6° Februarii 1946.

It was moved by the Viscount Addison to resolve, " That the meetings of this House held during " Secret Sessions of the last Parliament, and the Resolutions come to therein, be now recorded in the " Journals of this House."

After Debate,

The same was agreed to.

NOTE.—*The Viscount Addison explained to the House that the Resolution was moved in order that for historical purposes there might be a complete record of the sittings of the House, and that as there was no shorthand record of the speeches, and, except for personal memoranda, no record of the Proceedings in Secret Sessions of the House, only the formal Resolutions passed in the House should be recorded in the Journals.*

Record of Secret Sessions.

NOTE.—*The House sat in the Chamber of the House of Lords, except when it sat in the Annexe, until the Chamber of the House of Commons was entirely destroyed by fire in the air raid on the night of 10th May 1941, when the House, having expressed their willingness to place the Chamber appropriated to their use at the disposal of the House of Commons, His Majesty the King gave directions that it should be made available for their sittings. The House then sat in the temporary Chamber arranged in the King's Robing Room in the Palace of Westminster for all further Sessions, except when it sat in the Annexe. The House sat in the Annexe for Secret Sessions on the following dates : 21st November, 10th, 11th, 17th December 1940 ; 23rd April, 22nd, 27th May, 11th June 1941.*

Session 1939–1940.

1940 : 20th June ; 24th July ; 17th, 18th September ; 8th, 15th, 16th October.

Session 1940–1941.

1940 : 24th October ; 6th, 12th, 13th, 21st, 27th November ; 3rd, 10th, 11th, 17th December.
1941 : 26th February ; 12th March ; 23rd April ; 22nd, 27th May ; 11th, 24th June ; 10th September ; 16th October.

Session 1941–1942.

1941 : 12th November ; 3rd, 10th December.
1942 : 8th, 20th January ; 21st April ; 5th May ; 16th July ; 4th, 6th August ; 14th, 20th October.

Session 1942–1943.

1942 : 1st, 15th December.
1943 : 19th, 26th January ; 4th, 9th February ; 13th April ; 5th, 11th, 18th May ; 14th, 28th July ; 13th October ; 4th, 23rd November.

Session 1943–1944.

1943 : 9th December.
1944 : 3rd, 10th May ; 6th, 20th June.

CLXXVIII

Notes

Chapter 1

1. Martin Gilbert, *Winston S Churchill, Vol vi – Finest Hour* (1958) p 860.

2. Percy Harris, *Forty Years in and out of Parliament* (c.1945) p.156.

3. *The Hansard Rooms* in The Times Survey of the House of Commons (1950) p 21.

4. Robert Rhodes James (ed), *Chips, the Diaries of Sir Henry Channon* (1967) p 273.

5. Guy Eden, *The Parliament Book* (1949) p iii.

6. *Ibid.*

7. *HC Deb* 5 ser Vol 478 c 2714.

8. B H Coode, Bombing of the House of Commons, *The Table* xiii (1944) p 100.

8A. A P Herbert, *Independent Member* (1950) pp 141–2.

9. HLRO file PO 313/13.

10. Arthur Baker, *The House is Sitting* (1958) pp 77–8.

11. *HC Deb* 5 ser Vol 495 c 967.

12. HLRO file ARP 8.

13. Harold Nicolson, *Diaries and Letters 1939–1945* (1967) pp 371–2.

14. *HC Deb* 5 ser Vol 417 c 1408.

15. *Ibid* c 1407.

16. *Ibid* Vol 379 c 1218.

17. *HC Journal*, Vol 197 p 96.

18. *Ibid* p 129.

19. Charles Eade, *Secret Session Speeches* (1946) p v.

20. Martin Gilbert, *Winston S. Churchill Vol vii – Road to Victory* pp 277–8.

21. William Barkley, 'The Press Gallery' in Baker, *op cit* pp 82–3.

22. *Ibid.*

23. Baker, *op cit* pp 83–4.

24. J F S Ross, *Parliamentary Representation* (1948) p 235.

25. F W S Craig, *British Electoral Facts 1832–1987* (1989) p 57.

26. Butler and Butler, *British Political Facts 1900–1985* (1986) p 243.

27. J M Lee, *The Churchill Coalition 1940–1945* (1980) p 41.

28. Earl Winterton, *Orders of the Day* (1953) pp 260–2.

29. Albert Vinton, 'The British Parliament in total war', *Virginian Quarterly Review* Dec. 1944 pp 27–8.

30. Ronald Butt, *The Power of Parliament* (1969) pp 170-1.

31. Herbert, *op cit* pp 140-1.

Chapter 2

1. Some Facts about ARP at the Palace of Westminster during the War. HLRO file ARP/12. The Regulations are SR&O 1941/757.

2. Winterton, *op cit* (1953) p.269.

3. Nicolson, *op cit* p.250.

4. HLRO file PO No 466.

5. Baker, *op cit* p.85.

6. Eden, *op cit* p.51.

7. Barnett Cocks, *Mid-Victorian Masterpiece* (1977) p.122.

8. *HC Deb* 5 ser Vol 407 cc 1084-5.

9. Letter written by House of Commons Library, December 1947.

10. *HC Deb* 5 ser Vol 416 c 2047W.

Chapter 3

1. Bryan Fell, *The Houses of Parliament* (1950) p 34.

2. HLRO file HG/8(7).

3. *The New Chamber of the House of Commons in the Palace of Westminster. An account of the Opening Ceremony 26 October 1950* pp 2-4.

4. *The Times Survey of the House of Commons October 1950* pp 5-6.

5. Robin Duff, *London Calling* 29 June 1941.

6. H. A. St. G. Saunders, *Westminster Hall* (1951) pp 13-17.

7. W. Sanson, *Westminster in War* (1947) pp 90-92.

8. C. Jones, *The Great Palace* (1983) pp 165-6.

9. Saunders, *op cit* p 16.

10. Jones, *op cit* p 166.

11. Greater London Record Office file FB/WAR/R/48.

12. Duff, *op cit*.

13. *Daily Mail Weekend Magazine* 12 May 1971.

14. Nicolson, *op cit* p.166.

15. Greater London Record Office, *loc cit*.

Chapter 4

1. A.J. Moyes, *Debating Chambers of the House of Commons* (1950) p 14.

2. Winterton, *op cit* p.272.

3. Baker, *op cit* pp.74-5.

4. Sydney Bailey, *The Palace of Westminster* (1949) p.14.

5. Alfred Bossom, *Our House* (1948) p.183.

6. *HC Deb* 5 ser Vol 478 c 2715.

7. Rhodes James, *op cit* pp.352–3.

8. J.W. Wheeler-Bennett, *King George VI. His Life and Reign* (1956) pp 616–7.

9. *HC Deb* 5 ser Vol 413 c 50.

10. Bossom, *op cit* p.30.

11. Saunders, *op cit* p.313.

12. G M Thomson, *Vote of Censure* (1968) p.202.

13. Herbert, *op cit* p 142.

Chapter 5

1. Robert Rhodes James (ed), *op cit* pp 405–6.

2. Nicolson, *op cit* pp 456–8.

3. Patrick Howarth, *George VI. A New Biography* (1987) pp 184–5.

4. Howarth, *op cit* p 176.

5. *HC Deb* 5 ser Vol 413 c 415–7

Chapter 6

1. Harold Nicolson, *Comments 1944–1948 (1948) p 57–8.

2. *HC Deb* 5 ser Vol 407 c 1006.

3. Baker, *op cit* p 35.

4. Ideal Technical Press Group. *Surveys* (1951) p 12.

5. Fell, *op cit* p.35.

6. Bryan Fell, *The Houses of Parliament* (1961) p 35.

7. *The laying of the Foundation Stone of the New Chamber of the House of Commons* (1948).

Chapter 7

1. Howarth, *op cit* pp 246–7.

2. Ideal Technical Press Group, *op cit*.

The four homes of the Members' Post Office

**The old Members' Post
Office**

**The Post Office in Church
House**

**The temporary Post Office
in the Corridor between
the Central Lobby and the
Commons' Lobby**

THE MEMBER'S COUNTER IN THE POST OFFICE OF THE NEW HOUSE.
ON ENTERING TO COLLECT HIS LETTERS, EACH MEMBER IS AT ONCE
RECOGNISED BY THE POSTAL OFFICER WHO ANNOUNCES THE NAME
ON THE LOUD-SPEAKER AND THE MAIL IS IMMEDIATELY
DELIVERED BY CHUTE FROM THE SORTING-ROOM ABOVE

BRYAN DE GRINEAU
HOUSE OF COMMONS 1950

ABOVE
**The new Members' Post
Office opened in 1950**

Note on illustrations

Most of the illustrations reproduced here are in
the Palace of Westminster Art Collection, the House
of Lords Record Office, the Commons Library, or other
offices at Westminster. The majority are Crown Copyright.
Where other ownership of rights was marked on the
original, every effort was made to establish contact and
obtain permission, but in some cases without success.

Printed in the United Kingdom for HMSO by Burgess & Son (Abingdon) Ltd, Thames View, Abingdon, Oxfordshire
Dd 0505819   5/91   C10   4235   3382/2   142612   Job No. 911030